MERCURY

MURRAY "OAK" TAPETA

OUTER SPACE

NORWOOD HOUSE PRESS

Cataloging-in-Publication Data

Names: Tapeta, Murray.
Title: Mercury / Murray Tapeta.
Description: Buffalo, NY : Norwood House Press, 2026. | Series: Outer space | Includes glossary and index.
Identifiers: ISBN 9781978574861 (pbk.) | ISBN 9781978574878 (library bound) | ISBN 9781978574885 (ebook)
Subjects: LCSH: Mercury (Planet)--Juvenile literature.
Classification: LCC QB611.T374 2026 | DDC 523.41--dc23

Published in 2026 by
Norwood House Press
2544 Clinton Street
Buffalo, NY 14224

Copyright © 2026 Norwood House Press
Designer: Rhea Magaro
Editor: Kim Thompson

Photo credits: Cover, p. 1 Elena11/Shutterstock.com; pp. 5, 9, 11, 16-19 NASA; p. 6 Vladi333/Shutterstock.com; p. 7 Vadim Sadovski/Shutterstock.com; p. 8 Zwiebackesser/Shutterstock.com; pp. 10, 14, 15 Artsiom P/Shutterstock.com; pp. 12, 13 Luca9257/Shutterstock.com; p. 15 Man kegfire/Shutterstock.com; p. 21 Gorodenkoff/Shutterstock.com

All rights reserved. No part of this book may be reproduced in any form without permission in writing from the publisher, except by a reviewer.

Printed in the United States of America

Some of the images in this book illustrate individuals who are models. The depictions do not imply actual situations or events.

CPSIA compliance information: Batch #CSNHP26: For further information contact Norwood House Press at 1-800-237-9932.

TABLE OF CONTENTS

Where Is Mercury?..4

How Was Mercury Discovered?................................8

What Is It Like on Mercury?..10

Has Mercury Been Explored?..18

Glossary...22

Thinking Questions...23

Index..24

About the Author..24

Where Is Mercury?

Our **solar system** has eight planets. Mercury is closest to the Sun. It is about 36 million miles (58 million kilometers) away from the Sun. It is a bit larger than Earth's moon.

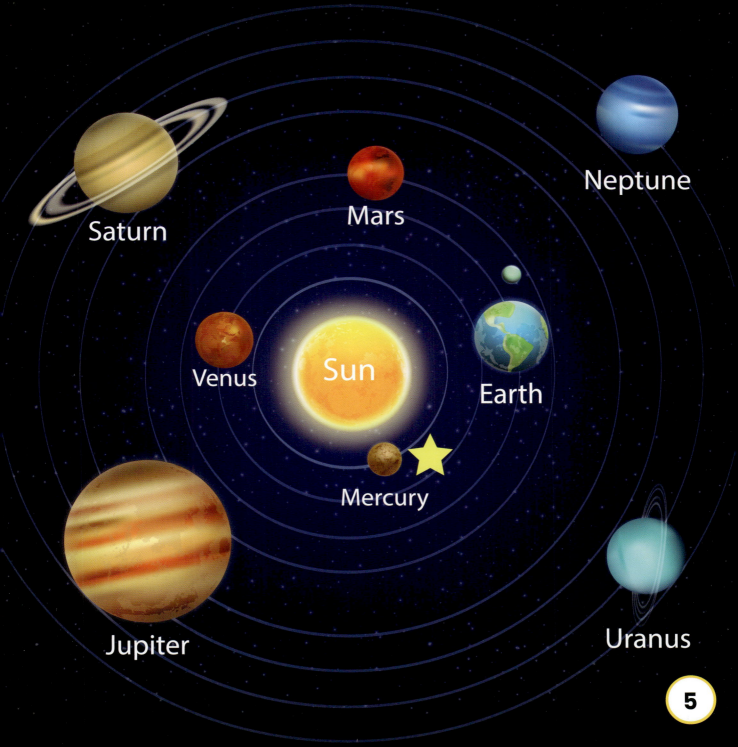

A year on Mercury lasts 88 Earth days. This is how long it takes the planet to **orbit** the Sun.

Compared to the other planets, Mercury's orbit is fast. Earth's orbit takes more than four times as long. Mercury is called "the swift planet."

How Was Mercury Discovered?

Ancient people noticed Mercury among the stars. They saw how quickly it moved across the sky. They named the planet after the Roman god of speed.

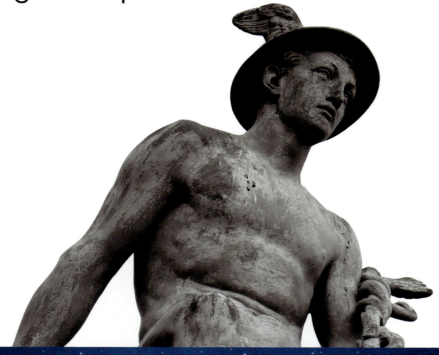

Mercury was first viewed through a **telescope** in 1609. It was seen by Italian **astronomer** Galileo Galilei. It was also seen by English astronomer Thomas Harriot.

What Is It Like on Mercury?

Mercury is a **terrestrial** planet. It is dry and rocky. The surface is covered by gray dust.

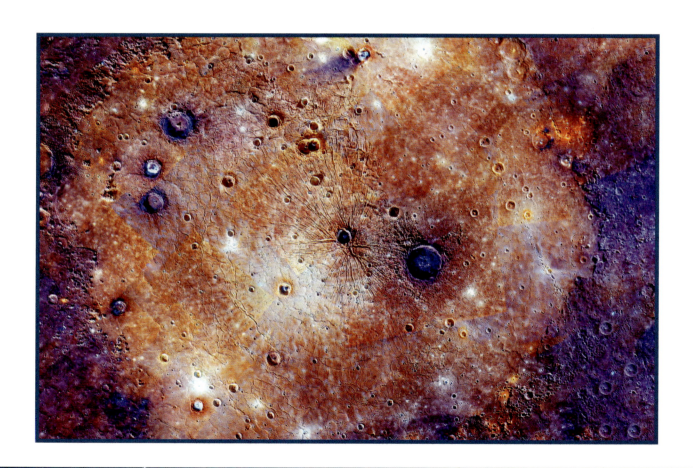

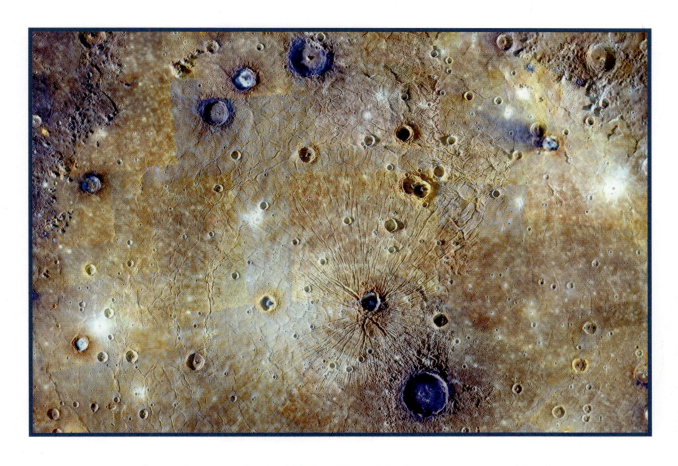

Mercury looks a lot like Earth's moon. It has many **craters**. The biggest crater is Caloris Basin. It would span the distance between New York City and Chicago.

Mercury is closer to the Sun than Earth is. The Sun looks three times larger from Mercury than it does from Earth.

Gravity on Mercury is weaker than it is on Earth. On Mercury, you could jump over five feet (one and one-half meters) into the air!

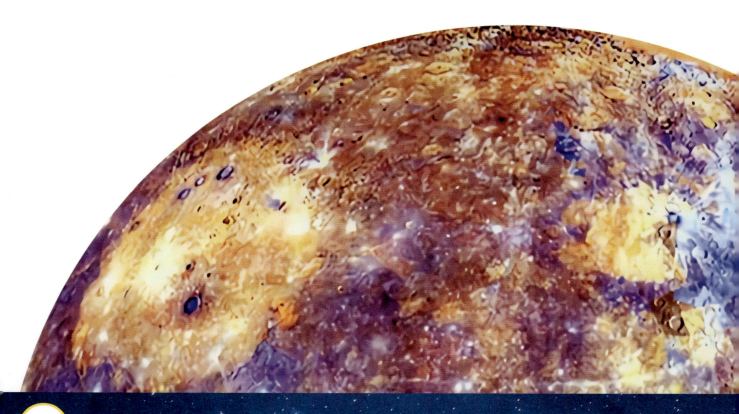

Mercury has no **atmosphere**. It is not protected from the Sun. It is not protected from outer space. It gets very hot and very cold.

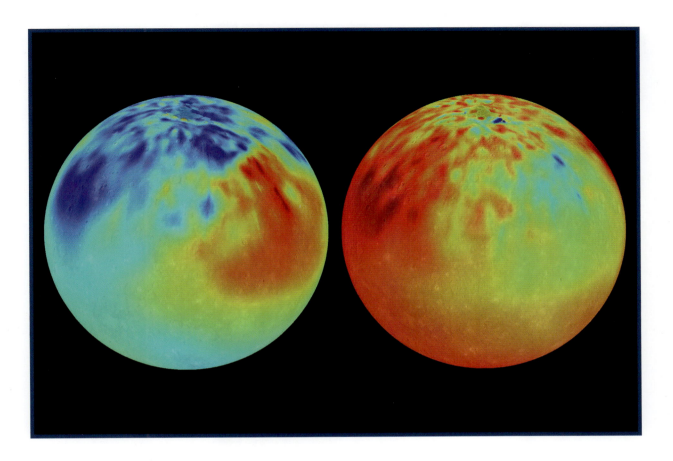

The side that faces the Sun can be 800 degrees Fahrenheit (427 degrees Celsius). The side that faces away from the Sun can be −290 degrees Fahrenheit (−179 degrees Celsius).

Has Mercury Been Explored?

Mercury is the least explored planet in our solar system. In 1974, the **satellite** *Mariner 10* took photos of Mercury.

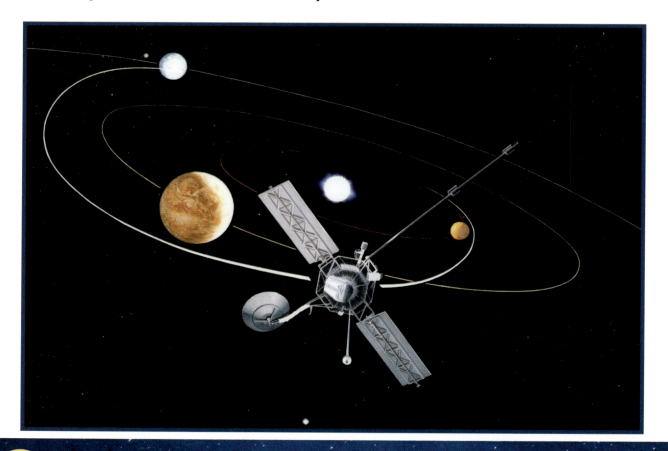

In 2004, the satellite *MESSENGER* went to Mercury. *BepiColombo* left Earth in 2018. It reached Mercury in 2025.

Humans could not live on Mercury. But people are still curious about the swift planet. Scientists study it to learn more about our solar system.

Glossary

astronomer (uh-STRAH-nuh-mer): a scientist who studies objects in the sky, including planets, galaxies, and stars

atmosphere (AT-muhs-feer): the mixture of gases that surrounds a planet; air

craters (KRAY-turz): large holes in the ground caused by the impact of something falling or exploding, such as a meteorite crashing or a volcano erupting

gravity (GRAV-i-tee): an invisible force that pulls objects toward each other and keeps them from floating away

orbit (OR-bit): to follow a curved path around a larger body in space

satellite (SAT-uh-lite): a spacecraft sent into orbit around a planet, moon, or other object in space

solar system (SOH-lur SIS-tuhm): the Sun and everything that orbits around it

telescope (TEL-uh-skope): an instrument that helps people see distant objects

terrestrial (tuh-RES-tree-uhl): made up of rocks or metals and having a hard surface

Thinking Questions

1. How did the planet Mercury get its name?

2. Describe the surface of Mercury.

3. Why does Mercury get so hot and so cold?

4. In what ways is Mercury like Earth's moon?

5. Why do scientists want to study Mercury?

Index

BepiColombo 19

Caloris Basin 11

Earth 4, 7, 11, 13, 14, 19

Galilei, Galileo 9

gravity 14

orbit 6, 7

satellite 18, 19

Sun 4, 6, 13, 16, 17

surface 10

temperature 16, 17

About the Author

Murray "Oak" Tapeta was born in a cabin without plumbing in Montana. Growing up in the great outdoors, he became a lover of nature. He earned the nickname "Oak" after climbing to the top of an oak tree at the age of three. Oak loves to read and write. He has written many books about events in history and other subjects that fascinate him. He prefers spending time in the wilderness with his dog Birchy.